WHISPERS & DREAMS

THE COLLECTED POEMS OF
KEVIN F.J. HARRIS

Polar Bear Scribbles
from Kevin F.J. Harris

Whispers & Dreams

First Edition, May 2022

ISBN: 9-798807-189028

Typography:
Cormorant Unicase
Adobe Jenson Pro

Cover design by Kevin F.J. Harris.

FOR APRIL

*No one's heart will ever be truer
to yours than mine. No matter
where God leads us — I am, and
ever shall be, yours.*

Contents

Contents cont'd

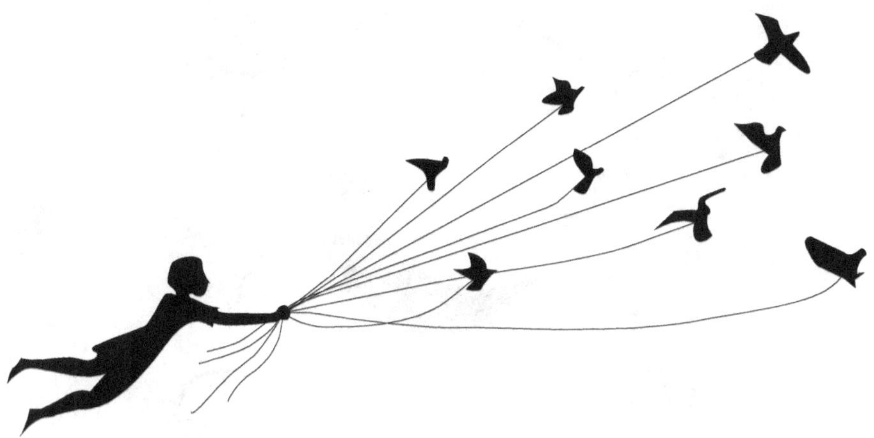

Prologue

Ever since I was a teenager I have suffered from a disorder known as RSAD, which stands for Reverse Seasonal Affective Disorder. I get depressed in the summer. As I've gotten older, it's gotten worse. But out of those times, when I feel like I'm the only person on earth; when I am dealing with the greatest despair, I turn to writing poetry and/or music. I will often sit down at my piano and just play how I feel, and take my sorrows out on the keys. Or I will put pen to paper and unleash everything I am feeling in poetry. In this book you will find poems written during those times, as well as times of love, sorrow, anger, and joy. These poems represent my very soul, and I hope you enjoy delving into the emotional maelstrom of my life.

If you suffer from depression, don't ever lose your grasp on hope, don't let it fly away. Hold on with all you have and reach out to those who love you for support. Life is wonderful, but it can be hard. But if life was easy, it would be pretty boring. I wish you all the best!

Loneliness

When I think of her, I can't help but shed a tear,
I'll never get to hold her hand or feel her warmth so near,
I remember all the memories of times we had,
through thick and thin, through good and bad.

I lay in bed at night and look up at the stars above,
why am I destined to be alone, never have one to love,
every love I've had has crashed down around me,
I have so much to give yet I'm forever lonely.

I would love her with every ounce of my soul,
I would always be there no matter what the toll,
I see so many guys who take it all for granted,
they aren't good like me, their love is all but canted.

All I need, is one.
But all I have is none.
Loneliness is my only friend,
and thus I see how life will end.

Why must my life be amiss,
what have I done to bring this on me,
why do I walk this road alone,
why must my only friend be loneliness.

Loneliness.

Winter's Last Kiss

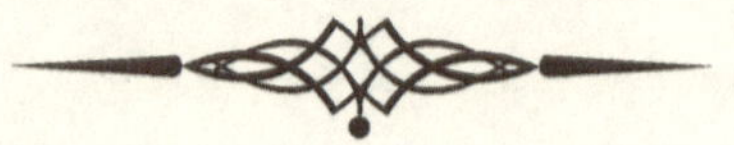

The last bit of snow is fading into the earth,
the trees are waking from their long slumber,
small buds pop forth as spring gives birth,
the days grow warm to me, oh such a cumber.

But today the wind blows with a whisper,
my sweet beloved winter gives a parting gift,
the air is crisp and full of that wintertide,
I deride at how spring by winter is thusly biffed.

She caresses my face and I close my eyes,
enraptured by her embrace, in absolute bliss,
her cold tendrils, her frosty touch is what I prize,
but this is her last tender touch, winter's last kiss.

Into the dark abyss of summer she will fall asunder,
spring and summer's advances do I so spurn,
but winter whispers to me, "my love, never wonder,
for like the rising of the sun, I will soon return."

On that day I shall run headlong into her embrace,
tears streaming down my face, as I wait and contemplate,
my lover's return with the snow falling upon my face,
until that time comes, warmth and misery are my fate.

Farewell for now my dear, sweet, cold and icy lover,
I will be faithful only to you my love and no other,
My days will be filled with the bright, burning sun,
until spring and summer's tyranny is done.

I love you with all my heart, with all my soul, my all,
for in the fall, your first kiss will grace my cheek again,
and we shall once more be one, in harmony, in love,
and the world shall once more be your wintry domain.

Lament

I who am buried in deep sighs and tears,
my face suffused with sorrow, now with menace,
grows pale with remorse for days now past.
Grim images, dreadful shades, memories of lost love,
the lifeless eyes of those in my family, now dead,
the earth turns, ignorant of this lonely soul planted upon it.

Never has the sun seen one so filled with despair as I,
never has this world seemed so dark and so desolate,
everything seems to mirror my strife and sorrow.
My spirit burns no longer with joy or inspiration,
now just filled with ashes of a shattered existence,
anger and spite cover me in a shroud of hate.

Never will I feel the exalted pleasures of a blissful love,
instead my tears grow, just as when it rains,
this stream of sorrow swells with rapid torrents.
Woe is me! With terror at what the future will bring,
my heart lies frozen within my chest,
suffering in this way is too great a torment.

How can I ever relate, how can I reveal,
these feelings, this sorrow, this wretched existence,
this scene of endless misery and torment?
Seeing those who have another to hold, to love,
brings forth a well spring of hateful jealousy,
Oh my heart, it is for you I weep, never to know such bliss.

A cloud of mourning covers me, dark and black,
all the joys, all the pleasures of this life,
have now become filled with plaints and tears.
My tearful eyes and pale face, as if made of lifeless stone,
nothing but a sea of bitter tears pour forth from my eyes,
where once joy resided, now only torment reigns.

Who will save me? Who among you will love me?
Until then my heart in torment remains eternal,
weep at my complaint, you shades of Hell.
Alas, at its very dawn, the sun of my eyes has reached its setting,
I am the only one left, covered in tears and sorrow,
will no-one, among this lament, provide me with mercy?

Oh if only God would guide a faithful lover into my embrace,
then the clouds could part and the sun shine bright,
bringing the healing warmth of love to my frozen heart.
Then I would lament no more, no longer a need to deplore,
happy and content I would swim in a sea of joy and delight,
that has neither shore nor bottom.

How could so much grief be calmed in an instant,
who could so swiftly extinguish the flame of sorrow,
and bring a song of intense peace and joy upon me?
She who can count the stars in the sky, or the delights of paradise,
she who could exude within me rejoicing and smiles,
she who could behold me as her tender and faithful lover.

But always, whether her beautiful eyes were downcast or looked around,
they would gladden my heart with fierce joy and pleasure,
Earth and Heaven, among my joyful sighs, witness these loving hearts.
And through the serene air would be heard harmonious choirs,
winged cupids striking up such songs filled with sweetness,
my life would be complete, my lover and myself in heavenly harmony.

Continued ⟫⟫⟶

But those sweet thoughts turn sour as reality grips my mind,
I fall to my knees speaking fervent prayers and plaintive sighs,
could Heaven bless me with one whom I can love and call my own?
Until that prayer is answered in resounding glory,
the earth shall ever be dark and filled with unending torment,
Oh God! Dear Lord of Heaven, have mercy on me!

SORROWS

Among the darkness in shuddering torment I sit,
my face eroded from the endless torrent of tears,
the thorns of this lonely life into my heart has bit.

a quivering sigh of lament my heart does weep,
a questioning thought crosses the recesses of my mind,
this life a rising mountain, its path becoming far too steep.

if only there were another to walk the path at my side,
to bring the lofty burden down and comfort my sorrows,
but this life so cruel scoffs and with malice does deride.

I lay in my bed, no sleep comes, a pillow soaked in tears,
staring at the ceiling I wonder what will become of me,
as I think of regrets, failed aspirations, through-out my years.

No-one to love, no-one to touch with a sweet caress,
no-one to hold, no-one to care for in times good or bad,
so much love to give, it overflows among this duress.

But so full of love am I that a poison it has become,
eating away at a lonely heart, beating for no-one,
unless the love is given to the poison I shall succumb.

Oh the toil and misery I suffer so is nothing but a bog,
sucking me down deeper into the darkness of misery,
no light, no life, no love among melancholy's blinding fog.

Continued ⇒⇒⇒⟶

Hopelessness fills me with an unending chorus,
singing a song of sorrows and lamentations,
full of tears, shuddering in wailing, my voice hoarse.

That feared day of wrath and doom comes impending,
when from Heaven my Father and judge descends,
Earth splitting in two and in fiery ashes comes the ending.

Without another to walk with, my time falling and growing empty,
on that day of death with nature quaking and frail men shaking,
on the day of tears and mourning, my miserable life so petty.

But should there be a soul who can walk along with me,
then saved will I be from this moment of destruction,
I would shower her with love and treasure her with glee.

I would tell her everyday, every moment, of my admiration, my love,
my life would finally be filled with joy and overflowing with peace,
I would shout with such resounding as to be heard in Heaven above,
I give thanks to my Father in Heaven for this wondrous blessing,
there can be nothing more I could need nor could want in this world,
I would fall to my knees and with love and sincerity confessing,
With all that I am I shall rejoice and glorify you through my art,
I shall treasure her for every moment my lungs draw breath,
I shall worship her and love her always, until death do us part.

But these are just dreams, and my head now falls low,
the reality returns and my sorrow resumes unabated,
angry and raging, wishing for a thing never makes it so.

No wondrous blessing of a kind and gentle woman to love and call my own,
only torment and sorrow raining down upon me in unending torrents,
my spirit crushed, my soul wrapped in lament as my heart weeps with a moan.

Winter, My Lover

I stand here among the towering trunks,
the wind blows across my face and I smile,
for I feel the whisper of my lover on the wind,
the chill I so crave with an insatiable longing.

I have had only one thought, one want, one need,
as I trudged through the sweltering heat of summer,
in spite of the overwhelming hell I endured,
all I have ever wanted was my beloved Winter.

I have longed for her return, to feel her cold embrace,
I want to spend morning, noon and nightfall with her,
surrounded by snow, ice and the sundering wind,
her arms around me, my warmth fading to a glacial chill.

My hands caress her face, turning to ice and fading away,
I want to fall forever in that icy grasp, loving her with all my soul,
when spring comes that clasp shall be broken,
and she will drift away, with icy tears, we'll once again be apart.

But for now I will wrap myself in that white quilt of snow,
feeling myself grow colder and colder in winter's embrace,
a smile will cross my face and I will know true happiness,
for my lover has returned and until the light of spring returns,
there's no end in sight and I want for nothing.

Winter Lament

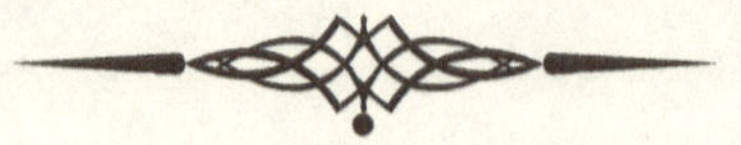

Sitting here in brewing angst,
a wretchedly warm winter, no thanks,
I dream of rolling hills in white,
blinded by the sight so bright,
frosted wisps of air a sweet caress,
embrace them I do without duress,
like death's cold touch brings upon a smile,
overjoyed like a child filled with guile,
but this pleasure has been forsaken,
the winter I love hast been taken,
ripped from my embrace in utter shock,
replaced by warmth an incessant mock,
I hate this winter truly an imposter,
set in place to scoff and fluster,
gone are the blizzards of old to my disdain,
replaced with tormenting torrents of cold rain,
the winters I love ripped from me asunder,
this depressing season pulling me under,
it shan't be called winter never more,
winter now autumn as climate soars,
I must take my leave of this wretched place,
so that one day I may caress and kiss,
the snow upon my face.

CRUSHED

Can you know this feeling?
Can you feel my heart?
When everyday is gray, clouded and dim,
when you feel tired and sad right from the start?

Can you know this pain?
Can you see these tears?
They fall from my eyes into an abyss of sorrow,
the thorns of life tearing into me over many years.

I am buried under the weight of dismay,
I am crushed,
darkness,
nothing but darkness and pain,
sadness,
nothing but endless sorrow,
loneliness,
no-one to love,
no-one to talk to,
no-one,
just myself,
myself,
drowning in my tears.

I Are Polar Bear

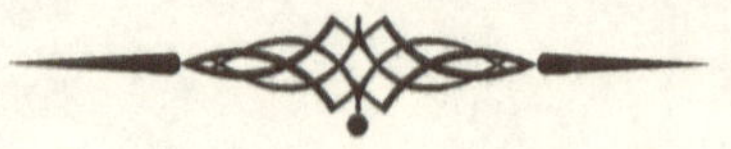

I need the cold which comes each year,
for the winter and I are intertwined,
when Spring comes I shed a tear,
for that joyful love will be torn asunder.

Nobody understands the life I lead,
what I endure with the coming of warmth,
I write what I feel, yet you do not read,
how much pain I feel at winters end.

A panic hits my heart and my body aches,
my head feels like it wants to explode,
all that joy of snow spring thus takes,
and my eyes itch, my nose runs like a waterfall.

Four months of suffering must I endure,
medication no longer working to resolve,
never leaving, always remaining indoors,
for fear of the poison that floats in the spring air.

My ears ring and pop, my lungs wheeze,
my days are spent wracked in dizziness,
only after days of rain can I feel at ease,
but so short lived is that pleasant refrain.

And just as my allergies begin to wane,
the next wave of pain comes my way,
summer's simmering heat bakes my brain,
and depression grabs me and won't let go.

The sweltering bile of summer does surround,
with air so thick it's like I'm swimming,
smiles and laughter from others does abound,
but I carry only hate and malice within.

Then hope is reborn as Autumn arrives,
crisp air killing all that lived to make me suffer,
gone is the pain, the heat and the hives,
replaced with anticipation of winter's coming.

And when sweet Winter does come 'round,
and she crushes the heart of summer,
snow and ice will come and cover the ground,
and my windows will fly open to feel her embrace.

I relish the cold, she is my eternal love,
we are one, without her I cannot endure,
when the freeze comes I thank God above,
for I live for winter, I need winter so nice,
without her I am nothing but misery,
I need to feel my skin turning to ice,
no longer feeling summer's hot vice.

I throw open my arms and fall into the snow,
I don't feel a thing, just the love of her,
you scoff and snort, you just don't know,
you don't understand, you ignorant fool,
I am made for her, my life does she rule.

No cold can vex, no wind chill can make me shudder,
and when the deep cold comes from the polar vortex,
and everyone else moans, cries and wallows in misery,
my heart is filled with resounding joy,
for that is when she tells me that she loves me.

Continued ⇒⇒⇒➤

For I am filled with the cold,
my heart is frozen in ice,
so many times to you have I told,
I relish the cold,
winter, no extent of wrath should you spare,
for you are with me and I with you,
for I are polar bear.

Winters Wind

It's a calm night, with a chill in the air,
I sit by my open window and wait,
for I know Winter, my lover, will soon be there,
she is the only one, my sweet, my mate.

The wind howls with righteous fury,
and the air transforms to frigid ice,
a snowflake, some sleet, Winter please hurry,
a white Christmas would really be nice.

I climb under the covers of quilted snow,
closing my eyes I drift off to sleep,
embraced by my lover you already know,
Winter has come and tears of joy I weep.

Icy tendrils creep around my room,
turning it into a frozen cube of ice,
curled up in my bed, inside the womb,
I dream of snowy days oh so nice.

I sleep so soundly in the sub-freezing air,
the wind blowing without end,
no-one could be happier than this polar bear,
watching the thermometer descend.

Oh Winter, my passionate frozen bride,
I love you with all of my heart,
At spring and summer with malice I deride,
I pray, Winter, you and I will never part.

Heart Shaped Cloud

Shining bright, fluffy white,
Heart shaped cloud is a happy sight.
Floating here flowing there,
Spreading peace and love everywhere.

You fly so high, up in the sky,
How it got that way, I don't know why.
With every year, I seek it out,
If my gaze befalls it, I dance about.

Heart shaped cloud, I love you so,
My imagination wanders, how far can you go?
Around the world in 100 days,
Moving north and other ways.

Heart shaped cloud 'tis your destiny,
To bring great joy, great joy to me.
Go on dear cloud make your rounds,
To you my friend, my love abounds.

Burning red, in the setting sun,
My ode to thee now is done.

Ode to Winter

I dream of the bitter cold, icy, air,
the winter wind blowing through my hair,
the crunch of ice and snow beneath my feet,
the gentle fall of snow and the sizzle of sleet.

I cannot stand summer's warm embrace,
I despise the feeling of sweat dripping down my face,
to walk outside and have my breath taken away,
the insects, the heat, it sickens me with each passing day.

I dream of my breath turning to ice,
because I find winter to be so nice,
to sleep with open windows in winter's embrace,
to feel the gentle caress of snow on my face.

I hate summer, back to hell I'll deliver,
I yearn for the chill that makes me shiver,
summer is utterly disgusting and vile,
it makes me so ill, I'll stay in all the while.

I dream of my face pink with the cold,
I love winter so much, it never gets old,
the crisp cold mornings with blue skies above,
I tell you most sincerely it is winter that I love.

Continued ➤➤➤

So begone hated summer, go and never return,
it is the cold biting winter for that I so yearn,
get rid of the heat, and the beaches can go,
bring me cold, bring me the sweet white snow.

Now that you know where my true love lies,
that it is the hot disgusting summer I despise,
never tell me it's a beautiful summer day,
I love only winter, so please, please go away!
November, December, January too,
February, oh winter I do love you,
30 degrees, 20, 10 and zero,
my sweet winter you're my hero!

Treasure

There is my mother, so simple, so sweet,
she has love running through her, from her head to her feet.
My mother is caring, noble and wise,
I just love to look, into her deep sky blue eyes.

My mother is short, but high in grace,
a petite little body and a beautiful face.
I love my Mom more than anyone could know,
her wondrous love is more pure,
more pure than the purest snow.

So Mom I wanted to tell you this great thing,
how having a Mother like you makes my heart sing.
I thank God in Heaven for this wonderful treasure,
having you as a Mom is a most profound pleasure.

Presented to my mother on her 60th birthday.

A Place Called Heaven

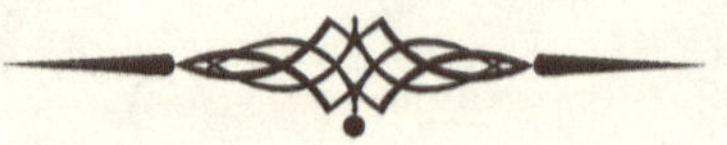

As the river's waters slowly flow,
among the trees a gentle wind blows,
my heart feels empty and my mind at ease,
sitting here among the willow trees.

The sunshines glint dances on the waves,
it is this peace that my soul most craves,
my hair flies with the wind's caress,
how it all came to be I can only guess.

I feel so warm, so free, so full of life,
no worries to ponder, no burdens or strife,
no fear, no anger, no sadness or pain,
I feel cleansed, after the morning's rain.

Where is this place you ask, where can it be,
where can you find it, this place I see,
I tell you it is within you, within us all,
through the buds of spring, through winter and fall,
through summer's hot days, among the robin's call.

It's the music I hear, it's the music I live,
it's the love I have, it's the hate I forgive,
it's my parents, my sister and all my friends,
it's my thoughts and prayers which my mind sends.

It's everything I have, and everything I don't,
it's all I will do, and everything I won't,
it's all I can give, and then much more,
its gates await us to walk through the door.

What is this place, this you ask of Kevin,
it's a little paradise, called Heaven.

I Yearn for Winter

I yearn for winter, with its air like ice,
To feel the frosty breeze I find so nice.
With flakes of snow bathing the world in white,
And the howling wind that blows at night.

I yearn for the cold and the nip it gives,
My heart sings for joy when Winter lives.
The skies so grey and all of nature asleep,
The warmth of the fire, burning in my keep.

I embrace the cold, the ice, the snow,
I love Winter, love it more than you can know.
Every Summer I wait and pray,
That Winter will return soon someday.

The dark evening skies, where stars abound,
That is where my dreams all can be found.
So do not despair or complain that Winter is here,
Instead be happy and show Winter good cheer.

So now I sleep in the hopes of its return,
To return one day, for Winter I yearn.
Spurn not my wish oh Winter friend,
Give me the cold, give me Summer's end.

Bring me icicles, snow, and sleet,
Bring me the crunch of frost under my feet.
I Yearn for Winter, anything else isn't right,
I yearn for Winter, Winter's warm cold night.

Hell's Dark Abyss

Chunks of blood,
fall like rain,
people's faces,
wrought with pain.

To hell's dark abyss,
they doth descend,
all hope is lost,
they've seen their end.

Heaven's eternal light,
does not here shine,
Hells eternal night,
blinding by design.

God's eternal light,
does not in this place shine,
Satan's eternal night,
suffocates with thorn and vine.

Their sinful days,
chance to repent long gone,
souls fallen and in ruin,
like the walls of Babylon.

No prayer will save them,
there is no parole,
eternal prisoners in hell,
bid farewell to your soul.

Continued ➤➤➤➤

Nothing to quench,
the pain and misery,
unending torment,
as you cry bitterly.

So save yourself,
while you have your life,
repent your sins,
be saved from strife.

Pride and arrogance,
will take your breath,
your soul marked,
for the second death.

Look to your Father,
who in glory reigns,
only He can save you,
from the eternal flames.

Then rise you will,
on that third day,
into eternity with Christ,
in Heaven you will stay.

You will know no pain,
no sorrow or tears,
only joy and love,
for an infinity of years.

Deny Satan's hold,
walk in the light,
or witness you will,
that eternal night.

Regret

I walk alone on this path of life,
it's been that way for so long,
I gaze upward at the cloudy sky,
and wonder if things will ever change.

With my mind at unrest, I pace restlessly,
what is going to become of this,
what will God allow my eyes to see,
why does He keep me so alone?

I lie there looking at an empty space,
my heart beating for no-one else,
how blessed this life has been,
how cursed this life has become.

I am to spend my days wandering,
drifting along the barren wastes that is my life,
my friends try to console me, to guide me,
but like an arrow, I must fly my course.

Every sunrise speaks their names,
those whom I have lost to death,
I could cry an ocean of tears,
and they'd never return to my embrace.

But hard as I fight, as hard as I try,
this anguish crushes my heart and soul,
and I cannot help but let go and cry,
I am broken, I will never again be whole.

Continued ⇶⟶

The thorns of life have wounded me,
the blood of my spirit flowing without end,
it won't be long now before my spirit flies free,
and the angels of heaven upon me attend.

Holding my broken spirit, I feel my life cease
"rest, good and faithful servant" they say to me,
I close my eyes and feel the purest peace,
forever with my Lord, my Father, for all eternity.

Never to have known love you see,
never to have had someone to walk this path with me,
never to have had that tender embrace,
never to have touched her sweet face,
never to have held her hand,
never to have walked barefoot in the sand,
regret overflows, regret overwhelms,
regret spawns great sorrow,
regret, for there will be no tomorrow,
regret, for I will never know what it could have been like,
to have been with a woman, to have been one with her,
to have loved and cherished her every day of my life.

Such sorrow.
Such anguish.
Such anger.
Such rage.
Such death.
Such regret.

Snowflakes

We are the snowflakes,
born on high in the clouds,
drifting around we wait for our time,
to slowly fall as wisps to the ground.

Some of us fall faster, some of us float,
but we all share the same destination,
as we go through our lives, growing,
meeting other snowflakes, making friends.

Together we float upon the wind,
for it dictates the direction we go,
as we fall through the air,
falling down as pure white snow.

And when our time has come,
to meet the ground and thus our end,
we touch the earth and are transformed,
from the snowflake, to water.

It seems as though our life has ended,
but that water soon rises again,
to fall as a snowflake, or drops of rain.

Don't be sad, don't you cry,
because there truly is no goodbye,
keep yourself calm, keep yourself sane,
because someday we will meet again.

The Bleeding Cold

There she stands before me,
tendrils of an icy chill flowing,
icy tears fill my eyes, I cannot see,
but I feel the touch of my lover.

Layers of garments she doth ignore,
as if I were naked like the day of my birth,
for her icy embrace I do so implore,
for she is all that I love and all that I want.

I smile and laugh as I feel that icy embrace,
oh it's been too long since I felt such bliss,
I wrap my arms around her, she touches my face,
I freeze, this penetrating cold is my heaven.

There is nary a shiver, no chattering teeth,
I make love to my beloved winter with a passionate kiss,
rejoicing and freezing my senses seethe,
cover me with snow, ice and sleet, it vexes me none.

The cold bleeds through me,
rushes into my veins, into my blood,
it freezes my plasma like a frozen, salty, sea,
she flows through me, turning every cell into ice.

Tendrils of frost seep into every atom,
she is now united with me and I with her,
sweet beloved winter, you encompass every stratum,
I love you with my heart, my body, my soul.

And as the light fades from my eyes,
I am submerged in the water of her life,
the cold water, transforming into snow and ice,
I find peace and my maladies now fade, in her embrace.

I feel her tender kiss, her frosty touch,
she wraps herself around, taking me in frozen arms,
I have waited months, dealing with heat and such,
now to feel her arctic touch, her loving hold on me.

I love you Winter, I tell you I love you so,
while others cower from you, I run headlong to you,
that frozen embrace they will never know,
I feel joy and pleasure when you are with me,
and utter sorrow when in Spring you are forced to go,
through summers torment, hate and spite,
when you return again, the suffering fades,
my lover has returned for me to behold,
and I am at peace, filled with happiness and joy,
to once more feel that love, to feel the cold.

No. 1

So many years I lay alone at night,
so many years I prayed with all my might,
that God would bring me someone to love.

So many years did I cry, my heart so lonely I could die,
wishing I could spend my life with someone.
So many years went past, I didn't know how long I could last,
with no-one to embrace, no-one to kiss.

I think of what has happened, I think of the loss I have been through,
thinking that was all there was for me to endure.
Now times have changed, it's something God has arranged,
someone for me to care for once more.

So many feelings fill my mind, so many feelings fill my heart,
when I think about you, think about how beautiful you are.
So many feelings overwhelm me, so many feelings make me smile,
when I hear your voice, hear that voice that takes me far away.

Now could this be my prayers coming true,
that I was meant to be with you,
perhaps as long as a lifetime?

I pray to God it is so, that once again it is love I'll know,
to be with you always and forever.

No. 2

There was a time when I would wake,
and sigh at yet another day alone,
I felt there was no difference I could make,
so melancholy would make me depression prone.

I thought I would spend every waking hour,
a miserable and lonely being,
My outlook on life was bleak and sour,
it just wasn't worth seeing.

Then a door opened before my eyes,
a brightness shone within,
I almost thought surely I had died,
but little did I know what I was to win.

You came into my life like a jolt,
lightning striking my heart,
Against the loneliness a revolt,
with you I could never part.

Your sweet voice, your heavenly face,
it brought me back to life,
I yearn for the day I feel your embrace,
and the end to all my strife.

My heart swells and swells,
with the love I have for you,
I wait for the day we can tell,
each other, I do.

Continued ⟶

My love runs wild, my love runs deep,
down into my lonely soul,
I hope it is your heart I can keep,
and for me to play my role.

I thank almighty God in heaven,
and the angels far above,
I am yours, I am your Kevin,
and you are mine to love.

No. 3

The time is coming when we will meet,
My anxiety is peaking, I'm getting cold feet,
Let me tell you about all the ways,
That I will be feeling over the next few days.

With four days to go, I cannot wait,
the feelings are stirring, you can relate.
With three days left, excitement will be growing,
Toward you my dearest, I will be going.

With two days remaining, I will be all nerves,
But I will give you all the love and respect you deserve.
With one day waiting, I'll be quaking in my shoes,
but soon it will be okay, I won't sing the blues.

On the day I arrive, I will see you standing there,
I will be shaking, eager to feel your hair, your touch, your kiss.

No. 4

The day you came into my life will be cherished always.
An angel sent from heaven above for my lonely heart to hold.
My heart is no longer lonely, but instead
filled with the wonder of a love like I've never known.

When you first hold me, it will be magical!
A touch no other but my soulmate can provide.
Truly the passion will need no words.
Your kiss on my lips is something I long for each day.

With a single kiss the intensity of your love will be so incredibly clear!
I pray your eyes melt me with emotion so intense it is beyond belief.
A caring and unconditional love will shine from them
making me shiver with excitement for our life to come.

I pray your smile fills my heart with a joy like no other.
Oh but to have you in my life is truly a blessing!
On the day we wed…
I promise to you yet again my unconditional love and devotion.

For I will cherish each day that God gives me with you,
our own little piece of heaven on earth.
I will love you always.

No. 5

A tear leaves my eye as through the air I fly,
as I leave you far behind me,
I feel a lump in my throat, my heart breaking,
I cannot wait to feel your embrace again.

I remember all that we shared the past few days,
I know more now than I ever did, I know now that I love you,
even more than before.

I miss you more than anything, miss your kiss, your touch,
I know we will meet again soon, but it will be a painful wait,
and when that day comes I shall embrace you, my
passion will overtake you, and we will be one again.

No. 6

I have found a treasure, a treasure unlike any in the world,
for years I sought,
for countless nights I lie awake,
for so long I wondered
if my life would be spent alone.

Then when I least expected it, the treasure found me,
for weeks I have been enraptured,
for countless nights I have slept soundly,
knowing that this treasure, this love, had finally found me.

It is you.
It is everything that makes you who you are.
It is your laugh.
It is the sparkle of the sun in your eyes and the soft caress of your touch.
It is the sound of my name on your lips and my lips sweetly kissing you.

It is your strength of will and your wisdom.
It is everything that you are.
It is love.

Now come with me, take my hand, walk with me to the ends of the Earth,
feel my warmth, feel the love, oh the overflowing love I have to give,
take it and embrace it.

Walk with me through the streets, the rolling hills,
the valleys and the mountains,
take me to the sea with the spray of salt in the air,
take me to the fire of the earth, to the blue sky and white clouds,
walk with me in the clouds, down to Earth again,
run through the wild flowers with me,
your beauty cannot be compared to them,
look at me, know I am yours.

I am your treasure.
You have found me.
Never let me go.

No. 7

Last night I had a dream, that I had met someone special,
that I had met the woman of my dreams.
Her hair was long and soft and her eyes blue as the sky,
her skin was as soft as silk.

Her face was as beautiful as the most beautiful flower,
and her voice was as sweet as honey.
Our lips met and it was like heaven, I embraced her and
never wanted to let her go.

I dreamt my prayers had been answered, that I finally found
someone to love and to cherish.
But then I woke up and stared at the ceiling, I began to panic.
Had this been but a dream, was I alone again?

No.

It was real, you are my sweet love and my dream come true.
But most of all, more than anything else, my heart cries out,
that deep within my soul, deep within my being I know,
how much I love you.

I want to wake up from my dreams every morning and see your
shining face, lying there next to me.
I want to see the sun's early beams light up your beauty to make you
look like an angel from heaven.

You are my angel,
my all,
my everything,
my soulmate,
my sweet love,
a gift sent from above.

This distance which separates us doesn't matter,
for my love goes beyond the boundaries of miles, time and space.

My heart yearns to be with you,
to feel your caress,
to feel your kiss,
to inhale your sweet scent,
to bring my name to your lips,
in the throws of passion.

I want to be your all, your everything, I want to love you forever,
I will love you forever and I will always be yours to cherish and to hold,
to caress, to kiss, to love.

I love you.

No. 8

I lie in bed, gazing out of the window, and see a shining star,
It makes me think of you, my love,
You are my shining star, far out in the distance,
no matter how far you are, your light is always shining on me.

I would do anything to bathe in your brightness, your light and warmth,
I would build a spaceship to fly into your arms and kiss your lips again,
My life orbits around you, the center of my universe.
I feel your pull, you feel mine, and soon we shall embrace and never part.

I yearn to be with you my shining star, twinkling ever so far,
no matter where I am, no matter where you go,
your light will always shine on me
and my love will always shine on you.

In time you will come down to Earth, my angel from the heavens,
we shall be united in love and trust, in faith and in union with God,
we shall love one another for all time, my star, my angel, my love.

No. 9

I hold your photo in my hands, I caress it gently, I smile and look at you
frozen in time,
I know that you are there my love, just very far away.

My heart aches to be with you,
to hold you,
to hear your voice,
to hear your laugh,
to see your smile,
to see your sparkling eyes,
to feel you near me,
to kiss your sweet lips,
to tell you just how much I love you.

I feel so special, so alive when I am near you,
you are my sunlight, my refreshing water on a hot day,
you are my hot chocolate among the icy snow,
you are my soul-mate, you are my love,
you are everything to me.

When we are apart I wilt and fade,
my life goes back to being just another day,
but when the phone rings and I hear your voice,
I come to life, my heart sings and a smile crosses my face,
I need you, you need me, we are two halves of a whole being.

I cannot wait to be with you always.
I cannot wait to hold you every day, to kiss you every night,
to hear your voice when I wake and before I close my eyes,
to dream of you and I living happily ever after.

No. 10

I yearn for the gentle breeze which caresses my ears,
for it is your most angelic voice I so long to hear,
your name is a whisper at every turn upon my breath,
I say I want to be with you until parted by death,
you are the one, such sweet serenity, your gentle air,
with my fingers outstretched to run them through your hair,
but there is nothing there for me to touch, only a sound,
but I know in my heart that a new love within me has been found.

You have such a heavenly name, such a caring heart,
I hope there is a chance we can be together and never part,
but should it be that our paths aren't meant to be together,
know I shall lament the lost chance, lost love, forever,
for once my gaze fell upon your angelic heart,
I prayed to God I could be yours, never apart.

I want nothing more than to awake each day,
to look at you and from my heart to yours to say,
I love you.

No. 11

When I think of you, I feel so happy,
I close my eyes and see your face,
I dream of being with you, beside you,
if only the dream would come true.

The blue sky above me abounds,
clouds roll by as the sun arcs through the sky,
I want nothing but to lie with you,
looking up at those clouds and to hold your hand.

Oh what I would not give to hold your hand,
to hear you speaking my name,
in the throws of passion,
to kiss you and tell you I love you.

I want everyday to be full of great joy,
I want to embrace every challenge at your side,
together nothing could stand in our way,
for nothing can defeat two hearts beating as one.

Without you I am but half a person,
my heart beats alone in my chest,
without you the days seem just ordinary,
I want everyday to be special.

Long has my soul lamented the lonely days,
long has my heart sorrowfully beat in my chest,
long have I been without someone to hold,
but waiting for you has been worth it.

Continued ⋙⟶

I can think of no-one else I'd rather love,
I cannot imagine life without you,
but if another's embrace is what you seek,
then I must continue my quest for my second half.

But should you choose me, I will not disappoint,
I will strive to live every moment for you,
I will do all I can to make each day a happy one,
I shall always and forever be yours and yours alone.

You needn't worry about love betrayed,
for once my heart is given to you,
it can belong to no-one else,
my soul, my God do not allow me to waver.

I give myself fully to you,
to hold,
to kiss,
to have,
to love,
eternally.

No. 12

Rest your head and close your eyes,
everything will be okay,
know that I am here,
know that I'm not far away.

Feel at ease and relax your thoughts,
I am your confidant, the one who loves you,
for as the sun rises on each new day,
know that my love for you is eternal.

I want to be your knight in shining armor,
defending you in every way,
I want to dry the tears from your eyes,
and to kiss your cheek and say
I love you.

Cuddle up next to me, feel my warm embrace,
nothing will bring you harm under my care,
let me gaze unending at your angelic face,
hug me tight, let me be your teddy bear.

Roll over and kiss me, wrap yourself around me,
my love will never waver, will never wane,
I will be yours forever, never to part,
I'll never hurt you, never break your heart.

Continued ⇒⇒⇒➤

Oh! What a blessing from God high above,
to have you in my life, day in and day out,
I have prayed so hard for someone I could love,
that the one is you I have no doubt.

I don't take what I say very lightly,
I think about it and pray for the answers,
I want to rush into your arms, hold you so tightly,
never to let you go, never to take this love for granted.

So when I speak those three words of love,
I speak them from deep within my heart,
I speak them now and they sincerely ring true,
my sweet girl, I love you.

In Heaven's Midst

In Heaven's midst I am, looking out amongst the dark,
Which we glide through on wings of steel, a mechanical lark.

Though mine eyes no vision reap,
into my God's hands, my life to keep.

Not a spark or point of light thus,
merely my boyish face in the glass.

So I sit, not any task or chore, among these souls on this journey.
Soon to be among those I adore,
soon to my Mother's arms I'll have near me.

Forget Not

My love, my sweet, carries on
with the pulse of life.
And though you are gone
your memory is forever within my mind,
traveling the endless cosmos of my consciousness.

I shall never forget the one who
was so lovely and dear as you.
With an essence and scent
sweet and fresh as morning dew.

My love for you is deep and runs
like a fever through my soul.
You may not be here, but you are never
very far, for you are forever in my dreams.

The heat of passion was never real
and could not be.
For you were another's, not part of me.

Forget me not, for I shall do
nothing in this world to forget you.
Dream, be happy, and always remember,
I was there and you were too
but I could never be with you.

Tides will go but always come back
when the moon is close
so shall I be.

Like the rain pouring from heaven,
like the winds of time never ending,
please dear sweet,
forget not the one who loved you,
the one named Kevin.

Fall

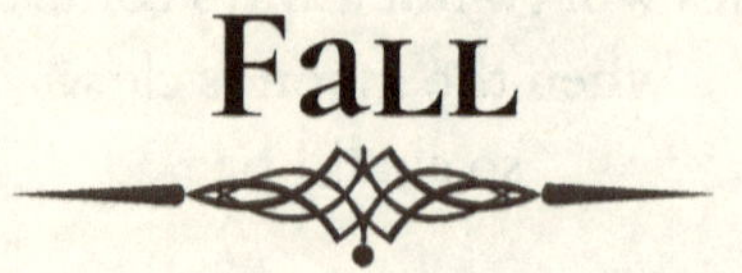

As the leaves of fall do die, so do I.
Fear not my heart, for we shall never part.
My love for you is strong.
And though I will die,
I shall love you for all time long.
As cold grips my bones, remember fair true sweet,
it is in heaven again we shall meet.

Coming Home

I close my eyes, bring my arms into a self embrace,
I stand in the cloudless sky, a cold breeze caressing my face,
tears stream from my eyes, falling down to earth as a cold rain,
my life has been wasted, instrument of death ending it I refrain,
I am trapped upon this heartless world,
a tidal wave of anguish and sorrow,
tries to wash me away, I want to give in and let myself go,
but the end of that will only mean eternal damnation.

I try so hard to do what I am asked, but this body and mind are weak,
they say I am intelligent, I can do these things,
they know not of what they speak,
my intellect is of a different nature, I am cold, creativily scheming,
I want to end these days of lonely existence,
I can't stop screaming the sorrow,
no-one to love, no-one to take care of,
without these things there is no tomorrow.
No one loves, no one wants, no one cares for me,
I should leap from the cliff into the arms of the waiting sea.
Plunging down into the infernal depths,
my life trails above my falling bones,
giving into the the cold embrace, of death, of peace, of eternity,
I have come home.
I see my Dad.
I see my Mom.
Grandparents.
Kelly.
Kyle.
Jesus, my redeemer.
I have come home. Free at last.

Birthday

I gaze upon the world around me,
I see and hear so many beautiful things,
a rainbow of colors for my eyes to see,
to all the songs that the birds sing.

The creations of God are amazing to behold,
and I'm so thankful for every living thing,
from earthy tones to colors incredibly bold,
and all of the joys they can bring.

But among all of the creations God has made,
there is only one that outshines them all,
her smile, her laugh, her voice a serenade,
a beauty beyond compare, proud and tall.

Her name is taken from the springtime,
when all the world is alive and in bloom,
her voice resounds in angelic form sublime,
her songs my ears voraciously consume.

So today, dear sister in Christ, I wish you a Happy Birthday,
may it be blessed by our Father above,
I hope to see you again soon someday,
and convey that it is you I so dearly love.

For April on her birthday

Empty

The rising sun,
has never felt so cold.
The green of summer,
has never appeared so dead.

The gentle breeze,
has never felt so harsh.
What I wouldn't give,
to see you again.

What I wouldn't do,
to see your face shine.
What I wouldn't sacrifice,
to hold you once more.

Each morning brings pain,
each day brings back the memories,
each night the nightmare,
of losing you.

This life of mine,
has never felt so alone.
This breath of mine,
has never been so shallow.

This heart within me,
has never sighed with such sorrow.

Continued ⋙⟶

Sadness fills my nights,
anger fills my days,
what were the last words I said to you?

I wish I could turn back time.
I would pay any price,
to feel the touch of your hand.

My turmoil,
has never been so unending,
my sadness,
has never been so deep.

My life, never so empty.

Friends in Love

My dear friend, my dearest love,
you are radiant, you are bright,
your voice is like honey,
sweet and angelic.

When I hear your voice,
I think I am in Heaven,
my ears yearn for more,
my heart beats with rejoice.

I know we must remain friends,
I know we must never embrace,
but that's okay,
having just that and nothing more,
is good enough,
to bring a smile to my lips,
and a twinkle to my eye.

As God is my witness,
as to myself I do know,
we shall remain friends,
until the end of our days,
always and forever,
my love is with you,
and yours is with me.
Every day will thus be brighter,
every hour will be filled with bliss,
every minute I will think of you,
and yearn for your gentle kiss.
I love you.

Kelsey

Quiet peace in slumber's embrace,
a gentle breath is all that tells me you're there.
Under the covers blanketing your face,
dreams in your mind taking you anywhere.

I call your name and the blanket stirs,
a stretch, a yawn and you soon appear.
Your eyes twinkle, I wonder where you were,
you're my best friend, to me so very dear.

I gently hold you, my dearest of friends,
and caress that silky soft fur that is your mane.
You sigh content hoping this will never end,
I will keep you safe, protected, from any bane.

Memories come and settle upon my mind,
of the days when you were so small, so new.
An undiscovered treasure you were for me to find,
an unending friendship, an unending love too.

Your eyes gaze at mine and it's me you adore,
I gaze back at you and see my best friend.
No matter what the days have ahead in store,
You will be at my side until our days end.

You are my best friend, my child, my life,
you make even the worst days fade into night.
I am your guardian, protector against all strife,
I do whatever I have to, protect you with all my might.

We are friends, we are family, you are my own,
you are my solace, my laughter, my whimsy.
I am your master, your obedience has been sewn,
I am your servant, your friend dear Kelsey.

Run wild through the field,
run as fast as the wind.
Run until the ends of the Earth,
may the rush never end.

Run with great haste,
don't let it end.
Time is nothing to waste,
run quick my little friend.

Run through your dreams,
run into my embrace.
Jump over streams,
with a smile on your face.

Run up the hills,
and down the slope.
You are my unending breath,
my light, my hope.

In loving memory
KELSEY
(2000-2011)

The Rain

Gray skies flow over me, the rain coats me in sorrow,
no hint, no sign of the sunlight, I am lost in the gray.
I sit here, desolate, in solitude,
longing for a voice other than my own.

So gray, such loss of life, the fire doused with rain.
The rain, oh the rain it falls unendingly, so wet and yet so dry.
The spark is gone, cannot return, the rain puts it out.
I walk the empty streets and see the places I once knew, as full of life, full of
the memories of days past.

I close my eyes, I see those I have loved, they fade away.
I remember the past, the fire of love, now ashes and dust, washing away
with the rain.

Will it ever burn again? My mind says no, my heart says yes, my eyes say no
as they fill with tears and fall with the rain.
The unending torrent of memories falling from my eyes and coming to rest
upon the soaked ground.

My most cherished love of all lies motionless, crippled, broken.
My prayers go unanswered, my tears keep falling, she is gone, hope fades,
the memories cut into me and I bleed sorrowfully, my other half,
flesh of my flesh, blood of my blood, into the dark, now a shell of who she
once was.
I try to tell her I love her, but the words fall on deaf ears,
I tried to tell another I loved her, but my own self I blame, my lover has
gone away, my flesh and blood has gone away.
I am left alone.
Alone, with the rain.

Men

So tired.
So tired.
Opposite of wired.
Under the covers I lay.
An abysmal reward,
nothing looking toward,
winter is gone and I'm dead,
winter is gone, filled with dread.
I trudge through the year,
suffering, turmoil, sickness, depressed,
dizzy, sneezing, allergies do jeer,
bright sun, hot days, summer's a pest.
Now here, the one time for relief,
but again my happiness is spurned,
I am filled with hate, anger and grief,
as I await, snowless, springs return.
Mother nature oh please do appear,
so I might crush your throat with my hands,
show yourself vile bitch, watch my rage sear,
as I destroy you and your vile warm plans.
So tired.
So ill.
All I ask is for an icy chill.
But wishing doesn't make it so.
I hate this.
I want to kill it.
Die vile warmth.
Back to hell with you!

How Long?

All I see is a world filled with unrest,
people complaining, pointing fingers,
all I see are people hate obsessed,
no love in their hearts for anyone.

All I hear are opinions, emotionally driven,
fear, anxiety, hate, and dismay is all I see,
people hurting people, no-one forgiven,
no remorse, no guilt, no shame.

A whirlwind of chaos swallows the world,
taking all our souls into the abyss,
if on the wrong side, insults and hurt hurled,
no one, no sibling, no family is exempt.

Everywhere, destruction, malice, and rage,
tearing families, friends, and towns asunder,
how long will this go on, I can't begin to gauge,
I pray that Almighty God will intervene.

Stop and think, are political alliances really worth,
the pain and hurt that you are dishing out,
is it really that important that you go forth,
without considering who it is you are hurting?

If only people could just love and love more,
loving unconditionally without anything else,
loving the rich, the middle and the poor,
and shedding the opinions in favor of love.

How long, how long, must we sing this song,
and watching the living become the dying,
how long before we finally realize it's wrong,
what we are doing to one another and this world.

Slumber

In slumber's embrace, serenity met,
I left my sorrows upon my pillow,
soaked with bitter regret.

Dead to this world,
enveloped in peace,
drifting in a world of dreams,
hoping it never to cease.

My breath fades,
and I depart this earth,
hand in hand with death,
from death to life rebirth.

I herald the clouds,
and caress the sky,
traveling in space and time,
to the place where stars die.

I've never held a star before,
my face brightly lit,
luminous and warm,
blazing and shining bright.

I let it fly free,
into the cosmos it goes,
splitting the dark,
sending it into repose.

Then something pulls me,
fighting it down I fall,
through the stars, the sky,
down and down arse and all.

Earth toward me doth rush,
clenching my eyes shut,
I await an imminent crash,
my fate I know not what.

A glimpse of my body,
resting in silent slumber,
the last thing I see,
anxiety turns to peace.

My body ascends with start,
and a sudden respire,
death's embrace broken,
my mind races in ire.

I repose, seeking slumber's embrace,
serenity severed,
more sorrows upon my pillow,
plaintive of having lived.

Don't Let Me Vanish

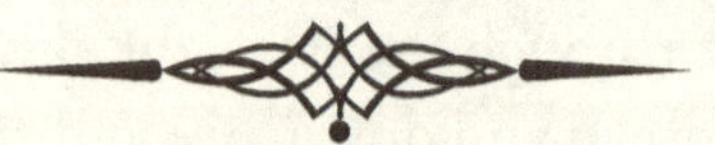

Flowing light,
glowing night,
stars dance upon the sky.

Singing trees,
dance upon the wind,
clouds fill up on high.

Swirling above,
a lonesome dove,
cries sorrowfully.

I'm afraid to sleep,
everybody dies,
what awaits me now?

I'm afraid to lose who I am,
death I want to rescind,
don't let what I am fade away,
don't let me vanish on the wind.

Happiness Eludes

Running, I chase happiness,
Like hunter chasing prey,
But it eludes me, it flees from me,
It's too fast and I can't reach it.

Moments of happiness try to come,
But the dark crushing night of my life,
Suffocates, asphyxiates, kills the joy,
And I stare endlessly into a swirling abyss.

Will I ever know true happiness?
Will it always be a chase that never ends?
I sigh in plaintive frustration,
The world around me twists and bends.

Upon the bed as I breathe my last breath,
a corpse overflowing with regret,
now as I grow cold in sorrowful death,
never to know happiness, only the eternal dark.

Does the deity I worship, filled with a grudge,
deny me this fluttering butterfly called joy,
on my sins so great does he solely judge,
this misery filled soul, battered and bruised.

Tossed around wave crashing against wave,
a storm of endless cacophony and rage,
anxiety whips me like a battered slave,
trapped and imprisoned in an emotion filled cage.

Continued »»»→

There it goes running as fast as a hare,
Happiness jumps and jolts from my grasp,
Breathless and tired I slump to the ground,
I scream to the heavens, my voice resonates.

Is there a God who would let me be so?
My heart clenches tightly in terrifying sunder,
my lungs collapse under anxiety's plough,
darkness closes in, where am I going?

Loneliness is a Friend

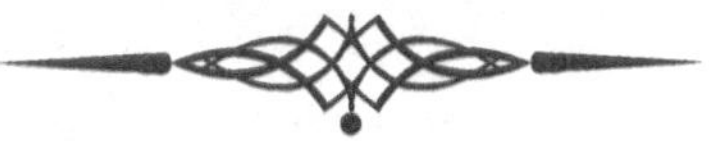

Silent and lying in wait,
a friend called loneliness,
no arguments, no debate,
agreeable but not seeable.

I have known it all my life,
drawn to solitude,
repulsed by the masses,
loneliness around me, a cocoon.

Nothing to say, nothing to hear,
a one way conversation,
no concerns, nothing to fear,
as I slip into my thoughts.

Like a leaf caught on the wind,
I wander through my mind,
hand in hand with my friend,
I rediscover the lost memories.

Memories flash, images fly,
some sting with sorrow,
some bring joyful tears,
loneliness holds me close.

I sigh a plaintive sigh,
memories vanish with the sound,
I open my eyes wide,
and see no-one by myself.

Continued »»»→

Staring in the mirror,
who is this person?
I reach out to touch them,
but my fingers meet only glass.

Loneliness turns on me,
my heart clenches in my chest,
sorrow covers and drowns me,
swallowed up and into darkness.

It was maliciously lying in wait,
an enemy called loneliness,
nothing but fears and regret,
I see it in my eyes, filled with tears.

Counterfeit Christian

Am I a disciple,
real and true?
Do I feel in my heart,
God do I truly love you?

Do I just put on a show,
a wolf in sheep's dress,
or am I for real a Christian,
unto you my sins I confess.

Where does my heart lie,
what is my true intent,
are my words straight as an arrow,
or full of lies, broken and bent?

Do I act like a Christian,
just to save myself from hell,
or am I truly a Christian,
my outward actions do tell.

I don't want to be the liar,
I don't want to be the fool,
I don't want to burn in hell,
I don't want to be Satan's tool.

Am I a counterfeit Christian,
As fake as fake can be,
I pray this is not the case,
I bear my soul so you can see.

Continued ⟶

I want to be more than I am,
I want to be like Jesus,
I want to be right with God,
And do things for him which pleases.

Lord Lord, please don't tell me I'm a fake,
Wipe these doubts from my mind,
I do this for you and my own sake,
Have mercy, and guide me home.

Death is a Color

Death is a color,
shrouded in sorrowful black,
red rose petals litter the ground,
blue corpses, never to come back.

Purple tinged lips,
a face white washed and wan,
a stone gray slab,
his name chiseled upon.

Pink are the eyes,
swollen and sore from crying,
of those whose loved one is gone,
a small piece of their heart is dying.

Brown soil heaped and piled,
upon this his final resting place,
death is coming for you, scythe in hand,
you can't outrun it, you can't win the chase.

Like wheat at harvest,
he'll reap your soul with unrelenting attack,
death is a color,
dark as night, eternally black.

Stone Tower

A tower of stones rises to the sky,
through the clouds and past the sun,
they rise so high as to touch heaven,
stacked carefully, stacked so well done.

Upon each stone are words written,
etched into the rock, with special care,
some rocks are jagged, some smooth,
words from the heart, a heart laid bare.

Each stone, a regret from my life,
and they rise high into God's domain,
they do not fall, or lean off kilter,
they are my guilt, they are my pain.

A tower of regrets climbs into the sky,
from yesterday, today and into tomorrow,
they rise so high as to touch heaven,
they weigh on my heart with great sorrow.

A Sweater in the Closet

A sweater in the closet,
hanging, bereft of life,
the owner long since gone,
a woman, a mother, a wife.

Reaching out I pull it down,
and embrace it with love,
tears well up and fall,
breathing in her scent.

A sweater in the closet,
a keepsake full of memories,
sky blue like her eyes,
soft to the touch, like her skin.

She has been gone a while now,
sleeping in death's bitter kiss,
all that's left is a sweater in the closet,
it is you, Mom, I dearly miss.

In loving memory
CAROL HARRIS
(1939-2017)

A Dog's Life

A dog's life, oh what a life it must be,
playing happily for some, others misery,
running wild through a field of flowers,
or caged up and ignored.

What would it be like to sleep all day,
to curl up and snuggle on the couch,
or to be abandoned on the street corner,
fur soaked and wet from the pouring rain.

A dog's life is what their human makes it,
filled with joy, love, and warm kisses,
or sleeping in an alley, shivering in the cold,
it is their human their heart so misses.

To be covered in fur with large peering eyes,
to run as quick as my legs can move,
to be loved, cherished, and cared for,
with treats and praise when my human approves.

A dog's life is truly a catch twenty-two,
one dog is loved, another riddled with neglect,
some in warm homes, others out in the cold,
many loved, many sorrowful with disrespect.

Sleep my fur babies,
sleep under moonlight above,
sleep my sweet pups,
and know in your hearts, you are loved.

Sleep poor abandoned soul,
sleep under the brightly lit moon,
sleep with my prayer,
that you'll be loved too, very soon.

Life's Waters

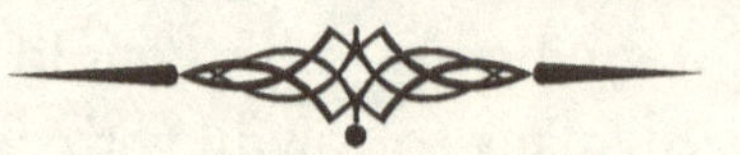

Take your bucket to the well,
Into life's waters dipped,
Sparkling with sunlight glint,
It is best gulped than sipped.

Differences

So many differences,
In this day we live,
Yesterday apart from tomorrow,
all the same yet different.

Deaf Rats

Deaf rats,
walking the street,
wandering in silence,
on their tiny feet.

Loneliness is...

Loneliness is a shadow,
Which looms behind you,
Ever present, ever crushing,
A spirit torn in two.

Loneliness is a weight,
Pressing down upon your soul,
Entombed in silence,
Buried in a deep, dark, hole.

Loneliness is tears,
Falling from a sorrowful face,
A plaintive heart filled with love,
Devoid of hope, devoid of grace.

Loneliness is death,
Scythe in hand and cloaked in gray,
It's cold, icy, grasp takes hold,
There before, and gone today.

Day to Night

Daylight snuffed,
blanketed in black,
stars like distant candles,
flicker to life, twinkling in silver.

Sun in repose, moon awake,
from day to night, switched,
from sane day life,
to night life bewitched.

Shivering Silver

Shivering silver, trees sparkle like glass,
Crystalline forms, delicate and brittle,
Dancing on the wind, breaking and falling,
Their time waning, so brief, so little.

I touch their coated sleeves, icy cold bites,
Slick and smooth, a watery confection,
Hardened like rock, sparkling bright,
Solid to liquid, dripping, falling, gone.

Sweet Girl

My sweet girl, wrapped in fur's embrace,
sleeping and sighing,
solitude and peace upon your face.

My sweet girl, you ran into my arms,
as if you counted the days,
waiting patiently for my arrival.

Sweet sweet girl, curled up tight,
I sit and watch you breathe your last,
stroking your fur, I wish you goodnight.

Sweet dreams my dear little one,
remember the good times we had,
and cross the bridge, free to run.

My sweet girl now runs in eternity,
as I shift my glance above,
I'll see her again one day,
for now all that remains is love.

In loving memory
TANGO
(2006-2021)

Heartless

An empty space resides where my heart once lay,
broken too many times, shattered and torn,
my very core lost, the price that I paid,
now nothing remains where it once beat.

I tried putting a clock in it's place,
wooden cogs and gears, clicking and turning,
but my passions were too great,
it fell to pieces, fell to ashes, smoking and burning.

I tried in vain to replace my shattered heart,
nothing could withstand this force of nature,
everything I tried failed and fell apart,
my head falling in despair, sighs and tears.

My heart is nigh, a pill difficult to swallow,
never to know love, cupid's arrows fail to hit,
nothing is left, just a space that is hollow,
now I am alone in a world bereft of love.

It's been replaced with a cold heartless wrath,
raging like a thunderstorm, blowing and wailing,
God have mercy on those standing in my path,
for no mercy shall I give, anger and rage prevailing.

Wounded by the thorns of caring and love,
I plow through this life, a dark storm unending,
I am the rain falling down in torrents and sheets,
a thunderous rage upon this world descending.

Heartless and bereft of care or concern,
anger and furor are the only things I feel,
love has been cast out, no longer to yearn,
a rotting chasm is all that remains where my heart once lay.

Heartless, a spirit broken and shattered,
callous and harsh, an open wound bleeds,
waiting and hoping to find someone,
who can fill that space, with the heart I desperately need?

Only a heart that is pure and filled with love,
rarer than the rarest gem, more pure than the whitest snow,
only they can rescue the wretch that I have become,
who will plant the seed, and help it grow?

Who will nurture it, and shower it in affection,
who will free me and break the chains of despair,
devotion, faithfulness, and gentle care, are all it needs,
to make it grow into a new heart, filled with love.

An empty space resides where my heart once lay,
a man shrouded in sorrow and regret,
a glimmer of hope shines in my tear filled eyes,
will the blessing of another come on this day?

I await that grace filled day,
and I look toward the heavens,
drop to my knees, and pray.

Tendrils

Tendrils creep ever closer, dark from tip to tip,
they reach out for me, to take hold and crush,
positivity, joy, happiness, they aim to rip,
crushing the light out of me, bringing darkness.

I swing a spiritual sword, my armor of the Lord glistens,
fending off attack after attack, slicing and slashing,
crying out to the Lord, and knowing that he listens,
I will not be taken down into depression's abyss.

The light of heaven breaks through the choking black,
unending attacks, upon Satan's shoulders lies the blame,
I fend them off with God's power and his Holy Word,
incinerating the tendrils to ashes with the Holy Spirit's flame.

Depression I am no longer your slave, the chains are riven,
I stand in glorious victory, toward Satan I do rebuke,
Glory to God in the highest, glory to him on high in heaven,
the armor of the Lord shone bright and victorious on this day.

How Do I Feel?

How do I feel, you want to know,
I miss winter, I miss the snow,
but if you really want to know how I feel,
sadness, regret and completely off keel.

I have so many thoughts running in my mind,
many bring tears, so many are unkind,
I feel so alone, in a wilderness so desolate,
I struggle and fret with thoughts that aren't true.

How do I feel you ask me again,
sad, angry, frustrated, in pain,
exhausted, depressed and alone,
in to the ashes of my life have I sewn.

All I want now is to end this strife,
not to hate each day of this miserable life,
to take in the blessings with new breath,
not to think of those I loved, taken by death.

Sorrowful tears race from my eyes,
summer's heat and bright sun I despise,
please bring it to an end, a quick refrain,
or at least cover the skies in pouring rain.

How do I feel, you ask me once more,
it is summer that I very much deplore,
stop asking me this, how do I feel,
just let me be, just let me heal.

Continued >>>>

My back have I turned toward God,
my faith lies shaken, beaten and clawed,
I wonder, where will I go when I die,
into heaven or in the ground forever to lie?

Maybe into the abyss of eternal extinction,
void of God and Christ, that's the distinction,
I fear my time on this earth is nigh,
that it won't be much longer before I die.

How do I feel, you ask in annoying strain,
so old and weak, in turmoil and pain,
I don't feel like doing any thing at all,
I feel so insignificant, so incredibly small.

So that is how I feel, that is my current state,
but when winter comes, this shall all abate,
all the sadness, depression, toil and strife,
will depart and leave me happy in life.

Bring me the cold, bring me the frozen snow,
bring me the joys of winter that I know,
and never let it end, never let it depart from me,
that is how I feel, now you know, now you see.

Here She Comes

Here she comes, with her long hair white as snow,
the ground beneath her feet freezing solid,
here she comes, the one whom I desire more than any,
longing for her icy touch and frosty embrace.

Here she comes, with snow falling all around her,
and the sun blotted out by clouds of gray,
here she comes, the one I've waited for day by day,
burying the world in a quilt of pure white snow.

Here she comes, the one I love more than anything,
whose frosty kiss brings me endless bliss,
Here she comes, the one for whom my heart sings,
a howling gale of frozen air, nothing better than this.

Here she comes, as the frozen trees split and splinter,
bending to and fro under the onslaught of wind,
Here she comes, here she is, my one true love,
Here she comes, sweet name upon my lips…winter!

Clouds

Do you ever stop and look up in the sky,
into the endless depths of blue,
do you stop to watch the clouds go by,
growing, shrinking, waving as they pass.

Wisps of white and gray hovering above,
like puffs of cotton and fluff,
shaped like animals or a heart filled with love,
flowing and swirling, sailing upon the wind.

Sorrow is an Itch

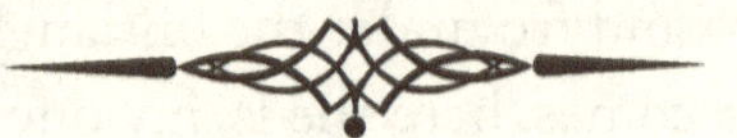

Sorrow is an itch that can never be scratched,
though we try, it persists through time,
never wavering, never ceasing, to burn and sting,
burrowing deep into the soil of my heart.

A Mushroom

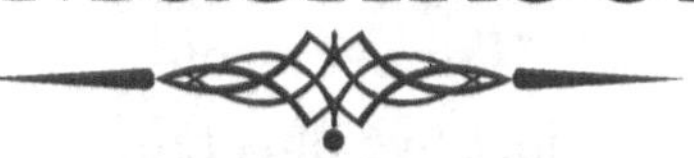

Across the field,
within the wood,
beneath the tree,
a mushroom stood.

Pearly white,
and oh so frail,
the humble home,
of a dark brown snail.

Upon it he sits,
drinking his tea,
looking up from it,
he smiles at me.

"Oh my, hello!",
he doth exclaim,
then quickly he hops,
and asks my name.

"Kevin", I reply,
he bows to me,
then he asks,
"want some tea?"

I shake my head,
tea is not my thing,
he smiles and sips,
his eye stalks swing.

Continued �》》》➤

"How old are you?"
he speaks again,
"I'm not to old,
just five plus ten."

"Why are you here?
he finishes his tea,
"I'm making a pizza,
for my friends and me."

"You don't want me!"
he exclaims in fear,
I shake my head,
"Not you my dear."

"Then what is it then?"
he asks, tea sips resume,
"I seek a beefy and tasty,
wonderful mushroom."

"My home you cannot take"
he raises his head,
I chop down the shroom,
he falls to the ground dead.

Gray Skies

Gray skies like cotton float,
deafening the blinding star,
muted and covered, a sorrowful coat,
spawning thoughts of blissful sleep.

Light dimmed and a silenced land,
all his creatures asleep,
trees like statues, as life is banned,
cold fingers stroke it with frozen still.

Seasons

Born in spring, tethered in place,
glowing in summer's heat,
falling to the ground like a race,
to rot in the embrace of death.

Winter's Cold Wind

It's a calm night, with a chill in the air,
I sit by my open window and wait,
for I know Winter, my lover, will soon be there,
she is the only one, my sweet, my mate.

The wind howls with righteous fury,
and the air transforms to frigid ice,
a snowflake, some sleet, Winter please hurry,
a white Christmas would really be nice.

I climb under the covers of quilted snow,
closing my eyes I drift off to sleep,
embraced by my lover you already know,
Winter has come and tears of joy I weep.

Icy tendrils creep around my room,
turning it into a frozen cube of ice,
curled up in my bed, inside the womb,
I dream of snowy days oh so nice.

I sleep so soundly in the sub-freezing air,
the wind blowing without end,
no-one could be happier than this polar bear,
watching the thermometer descend.

Oh Winter, my passionate frozen bride,
I love you with all of my heart,
At spring and summer with malice I deride,
I pray, Winter, you and I will never part.

Worry is a Weight

Worry is a weight,
crushing with crackling grind,
we seek and search unendingly,
for a solution we cannot find.

Pinned in statue form,
it eludes all common sense,
a vacuum robbing us of our breath,
a gut wrenching and unending offense.

Joy is Fleeting

Joy, a bird fleeting,
as I step closer it flutters away,
I'd easier catch a fluff of air,
or a gleaming sunshine ray.

Seeking and sought,
it eludes my every glance,
finding joy is finding sorrow,
an unending emotional dance.

What Happens Oh Death?

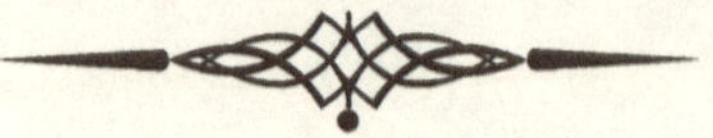

What happens oh Death,
when we close our eyes one last time,
thinking ceases, blackness shrouds,
a criminal act, life's true design.

All we are vanishes like dust,
lifeless shells, light snuffed,
we exude nothing but nothingness,
into a box like a keepsake, our body stuffed.

All that we were,
a memory so incomprehensibly brief,
for we are gone longer than here,
leaving behind flowing tears and grief.

Sorrow's Chains

My heart lies a pincushion pierced with loss,
each puncture seeps and sighs,
countless souls I loved have crossed,
rose petals crushed beneath my cries.

Tears a stream that cut and sting,
my breath runs from me in stride,
this crushing ache in torment rings,
wishing with them I had died.

If death had taken a cold snatch,
in torment no longer would I be,
with a puff of wind out like a match,
chains of sorrow broken, I'm free.

Christmas Eve Night

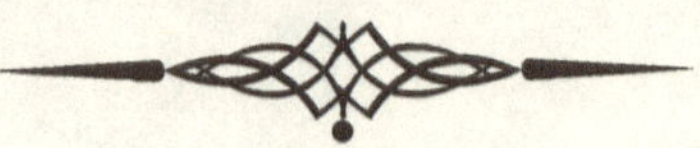

The night is cold,
devoid of any sound,
twinkling in the heavens,
stars abound.

It's Christmas Eve night,
with hopes for the day,
children filled with excitement,
for soon new toys with which to play.

A gentle winter breeze,
caresses my face,
as I stand alone this night,
staring skyward into space.

Wondering and praying,
for the blessings this year,
for my job, my church,
my families which I hold so dear.

But one star has gone out,
among the vast cosmic sea,
sorely missed, never forgotten,
this star was very special to me.

For unto us a child was born,
perfect and flawless in every way,
so think of Him and give thanks,
tomorrow, Christmas Day.

WHEN ACROSS THAT SILVER SEA I SAIL

When across that silver sea I sail,
leaving this broken world behind,
I pray before the judge my soul prevail,
an eternity in paradise will I find.

I walk through those ivory gates aloft,
and see all those whom I have lost,
for all my sins thusly and finally doffed,
by the lamb slain upon the cross.

What joy in that reunions embrace,
as I hold her tightly near to me,
to see her once more face to face,
my mother to hold, never lost again.

If my soul in careful readiness keep,
for God as my heavenly king,
no more tears ever will I weep,
nor fear death's ever somber sting.

Regret is a Spike

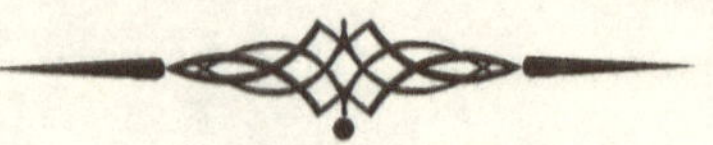

Regret is a spike,
driven deep into my heart,
knowing that I hurt you,
and drove us apart.

Weights crush me down,
as I contemplate my acts,
sorrow filled and tear stained,
it cuts through like an axe.

Remorse is a vice,
squeezing without refrain,
I'm so sorry I hurt you,
I pray you speak to me again.

Sleep escapes me every night,
knowing I harmed what I cherish,
I wander aimlessly in fear and fright,
hoping our love didn't just perish.

Dreaming

I close my eyes and drift off to sleep,
but rather than darkness what do I see,
a vast golden field surrounded by mountains,
snowcapped peaks and an endless blue sky,
I turn and I see the most awe inspiring sight,
you standing there waiting for me,
I walk over to you, your beauty gleaming,
you take my hand and we walk through the field,
you look into my eyes, I look into yours,
surely this must be Heaven, I walk with an angel,
you turn to me and smile, those eyes of yours so happy,
I tell you how much I love you, you touch my lips with your finger,
you pull me to you and an embrace ensues,
I smell your scent and your warm joyful heart,
I close my eyes wanting to stay this way forever,
you run your fingers through my hair,
because you know there's a little secret there,
when a woman runs her hands there I am immobilized,
unable to move, unable to speak,
you giggle because of this and push me away,
our hands holding tightly, I look back at you and smile,
we walk to the edge of the world and sit down,
watching the sunset you put your head on my shoulder,
I sigh with contentment, hoping that I will never wake,
but the dream fades to darkness and I open my eyes,
sorrow fills my heart knowing it was all but a dream,
but I spend my day thinking of you,
and it gets me through the day knowing that soon,
we shall be together again in my dreams,
and I pray to God that someday my dreams come true.

Lies

Twisted and turned,
your words hollow,
my anger burned,
difficult to swallow.

You lied to me,
You led me astray,
Filled with bitterness,
You're dead to me this day.

Don't try to fix your sin,
never speak a word,
I will no longer listen,
my hate and malice stirred.

I do not care,
I do not forgive,
within my heart,
you no longer live.

This hate I impart,
no caring any longer,
we will remain apart,
without you I'm stronger.

I will not speak,
I will not reply,
you don't exist,
this is goodbye.

Spring

Raging storms.
and thunderous anger,
my bitterness swarms,
like the furious sea.

Waves so sour,
and bereft of joy,
my rage devours,
casting me like a toy.

Jealous fury,
fills my core,
vicious hatred,
into me has tore.

Season of torment,
and my joy is gone,
suffering has hit,
I'm misery's pawn.

I love nothing,
Past pleasures dead,
sanity passing,
just sorrow, and dread.

Aching cries,
fly through my mind,
the dead haunt,
no peace can I find.

Continued ⟫⟶

Crushing weight,
unending despair,
don't cross my path,
into your soul I'll glare.

Raging and wailing,
tossing and turning,
eternal pain prevailing,
my mind ever burning.

I hate you so greatly,
and the agony you bring,
I'd kill you if I could,
and bring death to Spring.

Polar Bear Scribbles

POLARBEARSCRIBBLES.COM

www.ingramcontent.com/pod-product-compliance
Lightning Source LLC
Chambersburg PA
CBHW020125180726
47992CB00020B/2503